CROSSROADS COLLEGE

D0593433

Carey, George,

232.1   God incarnate :

C2733   MBC00000038265

Crossroads College
G. H. Cachiaras Memorial Library
wood Road SW, Rochester MN 55902
507-535-3331

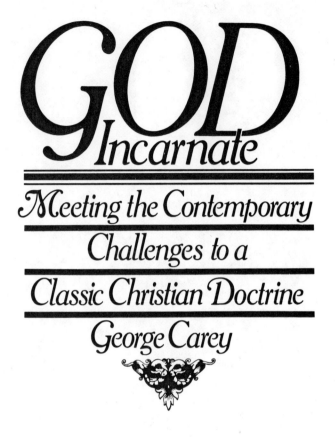

GOD Incarnate

Meeting the Contemporary Challenges to a Classic Christian Doctrine

George Carey

InterVarsity Press
Downers Grove
Illinois 60515

© *G. L. Carey 1977.*
First American printing, February 1978,
by InterVarsity Press, Downers Grove,
Illinois, with permission from
Universities and Colleges Christian
Fellowship, Leicester, England.

All rights reserved.
No part of this book may be reproduced
in any form without written permission from
InterVarsity Press, Downers Grove, Illinois.

InterVarsity Press is the book publishing
division of Inter-Varsity Christian Fellowship,
a student movement active on campus at
hundreds of universities, colleges and schools
of nursing. For information about local
and regional activities, write IVCF,
233 Langdon St., Madison, WI 53703.

Distributed in Canada through InterVarsity Press,
1875 Leslie St., Unit 10, Don Mills, Ontario M3B 2M5.

Quotations from the Bible are from the Revised
Standard Version (copyrighted 1946 and
1952, Second Edition 1971, by the Division
of Christian Education, National Council of
the Churches of Christ in the United States
of America), unless otherwise stated.

ISBN 0-87784-503-4
Library of Congress Catalog
Card Number: 77-27690

Printed in the United States of America

Foreword

The centre of the Christian faith is Christ himself. He is the content of Christian preaching and the pattern for Christian living. But who is he? What did he believe and teach about himself and his destiny? How reliable is the New Testament statement that he is God's Son?

These questions, old in themselves, have been asked anew during recent years by scholars, and certain lines of demarcation have been drawn up which separate the different answers.

The following pages should be regarded as an introduction to this debate, an introduction that seeks to put such questions to the New Testament itself. Did Jesus and his earliest followers really believe that in him God 'became flesh and dwelt among us'? Or was the incarnation a pious addition to the original teaching of Jesus?

I thank most warmly Mrs Joyce Lomas and the Revd Michael Heyward for burning the midnight oil typing the manuscript, and I am grateful to my colleague, the Revd Graeme Rutherford, for his helpful comments. Some I have heeded! Above all, my thanks to Eileen for her help and support. Whatever blemishes remain are my responsibility. In spite of that it is hoped that what follows will be useful to those who seek to know more about the One who towers over all time.

G.L.C.

Durham
July 1977

1
A Challenge

Jesus is always 'news'. There is an enigmatic, elusive quality about him which attracts the sceptic almost as much as the believer. Down the centuries ordinary men and women as well as scholars have debated his significance. Sometimes the discussion has been conducted calmly. At other times it has turned to passion, resulting in violence, as it did in Constantinople in the 5th century with the factions 'blues' and 'greens' locked in fierce conflict as to whether Christ's nature was one or two!

Through the debates in the early centuries the church, on the basis of Scripture, tradition and the consensus of Christians, finally settled on a solution known as the Chalcedonian Definition (451) that Christ was both God and Man, 'Perfect in divinity, perfect in humanity; truly God and truly Man'. Now, if we read the whole Chalcedonian Definition, we must agree that by modern standards it is lengthy, wordy and tortuous. The language is couched in an obsolete philosophy. But there is no missing the meaning of the Definition, however much the language and thought-forms have changed. It is saying directly that the church confesses Jesus as both human and divine and that this is the core of Christianity. The World Council of Churches is constituted upon the acknowledgment of 'Our Lord Jesus Christ as God and Saviour'.

It has been recognized throughout Christian history that the question of the incarnation is crucial to the Christian faith. Paul put it like this, 'For in him (Jesus) all the fulness of God was pleased to dwell, and through him to reconcile to himself all things, whether on earth or in heaven, making peace by the blood of his cross' (Col. 1:19,20). If this is not true we must face the clear alternative that we cannot know how to be saved, how to live nor how to think about God. We are left to struggle to do our best in the uncertain hope that God will accept us in the end.

This common understanding of Jesus has been under attack by non-Christians for a long time, more recently by sub-Christian cults and now by a small number of theological scholars. John Knox, John Hick, Dennis Nineham and Don Cupitt, among others, have played leading roles in questioning the traditional estimate of Jesus. Common to their different perspectives is agreement that Jesus of Nazareth was a prophetic figure through whom God acted. He was not in their view God incarnate in the classical sense but a man who became a supreme revelation of goodness and godliness.

Quite recently a new book has appeared, *The Myth of God Incarnate*[1] which has caused a great furore not because it has said anything different, or even better, than the writers above but because, with maximum publicity, it has attempted to focus the attention of the public on its challenge to the orthodox position. The preface of the book declares that it is written 'to place its topic firmly on the agenda for discussion'. It is therefore a deliberate and concerted attempt to change the landscape of Christian belief on the subject of the person of Christ. To give the writers of the symposium their due, their desire to do this proceeds not from an aim to weaken the Christian faith but to make it more meaningful to modern people. Their intention is to influence the church at large to revise its opinions about

Jesus; to take away the divine 'clothing' which, it is claimed, obscures his reality as a man.

This professed aim is important. The writers believe that first-century Christians were too much influenced by a desire to 'divinize' Jesus, to make him God. But the writers themselves are influenced by a desire to humanize Jesus, to make him acceptable to sceptical modern man. In this kind of enterprise there is always a danger that even a laudable aim might get in the way of presenting the whole picture of Jesus.

It is not the aim of this booklet to concentrate upon the arguments in *The Myth of God Incarnate*. Our purpose is to look at the subject of the incarnation more generally and to place some modern questions in a scriptural context. However, it so happens that this book does raise certain points which are typical of arguments used today and it will be useful to give a brief outline of some of its conclusions.

1. The idea of 'incarnation', that God became man in Jesus of Nazareth, is a construction built upon the New Testament and not found in it. It is, in fact, a false interpretation of the apostolic documents.

2. We must recognize that the idea of 'incarnation' is a myth. As a myth it does not declare literal truth but expresses the central truth that God meets us in Jesus.

3. Jesus was a real man born in normal fashion, a child of Mary and Joseph. He did not exist before his conception and birth.

4. The significance of Jesus lies in his 'faith-response' to God. His full openness to God expresses the full potential of humanity within his community.

5. Christ's Sonship can be seen as a development from the idea of God's 'man' to that of God's son, by analogy. The later full-blooded conception of God's *only* Son was a mistaken development.

6. Jesus is not different in kind from other men. His uniqueness consists, not in a special, unique bond with God, but in his capacity to inspire people to love God and to seek

his kingdom.

7. His death was a martyrdom which crowned his life and activated his mission. Traditional theories which treat his death as actually dealing with sin are dismissed by one contributor as 'rubbish'.

Add to this a rejection of the physical resurrection of Jesus (at least by some of the contributors), and the resultant picture is that of a human person, different from us only in what he achieved. The authors claim that such a Jesus, stripped of the mythology which Christian devotion and theology have dressed him in for nearly two thousand years, is not only more believable but more scriptural. *Believable,* because modern people find the notion of 'incarnation' too incoherent and implausible for words; *scriptural,* because once one treats the whole story without recourse to super-natural explanations, the true picture of Jesus begins to emerge from the text.

Our approach to the question contains three main strands, though not appearing in the same order or in each chapter. The facts advanced are at least equally capable of a tradi-tional Christian interpretation as any new one: a range of evidence which does point to the divinity of Jesus has been omitted: one set of intellectual difficulties (that Jesus could not be both man and God at the same time) has been exchanged for another set (that his greatness and the compelling power of his life is inexplicable if he were a mere man).

The Myth of God Incarnate, therefore, brings to the boil certain crucial questions concerning the person of Jesus Christ. If he is, as we believe, the very heart of the Christian faith we cannot be unmoved or indifferent to the debate. Indeed, we must explore some of these issues as carefully as we can, fully realizing that Christian belief is seriously affected by the answers we give to the ancient question Jesus once asked his disciples: 'But who do you say that I am?'

2
Jesus: Man of Universal Destiny?

The contention of modern scholars is that one thing we can be certain of is that Jesus was a man. So John Hick writes 'Jesus was wholly and unambiguously a human being, by race a Jew, in sex a man, culturally of the 1st century AD . . . we do not have to go beyond his humanity to find the Christian starting point'.[1]

With this many of us are in basic agreement, although his words 'wholly' and 'unambiguously' need careful study and explanation. Curiously enough, the New Testament does not go in for confessions of that kind. The fact of his humanity is more often on the lips of his enemies than his friends, who point out that 'Joseph is his father', 'his home is among us' and so on (Mk. 6:3; Jn. 6:42). The thrust of the New Testament, however, is upon his divinity; his manhood is indirectly observed through his life and behaviour.

His humanity is, of course, clear enough. That's where the disciples started in their understanding of him. In their eyes he was a real man, a man of their times, who spoke their language and shared their experiences. Yet, while this is so, and we must not diminish the fact of Jesus' humanity because it is crucial to the doctrine of salvation, we must guard against over-concentrating upon his similarity to us.

The New Testament concentrates upon his difference. This difference comes out in every stratum of the New Testament documents. It is there even in the earliest Gospel, Mark, where Jesus is distinguished by many factors, such as his teaching, healing miracles and authority. Now, it is well known that in the Gospels and especially in Mark, Jesus is reticent about claiming great things for himself. He avoids titles like Messiah, and Son of God. There are many possible explanations for this reluctance on Jesus' part. The writers of the symposium tend to interpret this silence as a denial by Jesus to be significantly different from other men. But it is more likely that Jesus wanted to avoid being placed in the strait-jacket of men's expectations if these historically determined titles were used of him. He wanted them to 'see' who he was for themselves. Anonymity was of the utmost importance if the 'newness' of his person and message were to be fully understood. But the difference of a person depends less upon what he calls himself, than upon the impact he makes upon those around him, and their confessions of him. To take a much less significant example, Mother Teresa of Calcutta has never, as far as I am aware, claimed to be an exceptionally gifted, charismatic, 'God-guided' woman with a devotion to him which outstrips most of us. But that she is few would deny. So it is with Jesus. The subject-matter is there even where titles are not used. He stamps his own character upon society and events and challenges in many different ways people's estimates of him. We find men in the New Testament constantly bemused by him and their views of him in continual revision. C. E. B. Cranfield, commenting on the 'secret of the Kingdom' in Mark 4:11ff., shows how the two motives of revealing and veiling are at work in the ministry of Jesus.[2] On the one hand, he teaches the crowds, sends out the twelve, reveals the power and compassion of God by miracles. On the other hand, he teaches the crowd indirectly by parables, seeks to conceal his miracles, forbids demons to declare his identity. His claims to authority cannot but have appeared altogether problematic and paradoxical. His authority dumbfounded his critics and, in their opinion, was blasphemy (Mk. 2:7).

But rabbis and prophets also spoke with authority; do we need to go beyond such categories to explain Jesus? Was Jesus more than a 'rabbi'? He also had disciples to whom he taught the way of life and he was called a 'rabbi' ('Master') from time to time (Mk. 9:5; 11:21). But Jesus' authority possessed a completely different character. His authority was not that of the derivative kind drawn from the Torah, neither did he, as did many rabbis of his time, parrot the teaching of someone greater like Rabbi Hillel. Indeed, in Matthew, the most Jewish of the Gospels, we find him contradicting the traditions of the Fathers and deepening the teaching of Moses (Mt. 5:21). The emphatic, 'But "I" say to you', must have been astonishing to Jews brought up under the Torah.

Was Jesus a prophet? So it seems at one level. He stands within the prophetic tradition, proclaiming the will of God, but even here he leaves the prophets far behind with his assurance and self-conscious authority. 'Thus says the Lord', the prophetic opener of men like Isaiah and Jeremiah, is replaced by an assertiveness which ill-befits a humble man of God, but is what we should expect from deity. According to Jesus' teaching about the kingdom, prophetic expectation was fulfilled in him. Even John the Baptist, the greatest of men and 'more than a prophet' (Mt. 11:9–11), was less than Jesus and one who prepared his way (Mk. 1:2).

Jesus presents himself throughout the Gospels, not first as a prophet, but as the object of prophecy.

Was Jesus the Christ, the 'Messiah' of God? Jesus never claims this title for himself although it is attributed to him by others, and he acknowledged it, on oath, at his trial. But his ministry is meaningless unless he firmly believed that he was God's chosen one to redeem his people. In fact, no sense can be made of Jesus himself unless we are prepared to acknowledge that Jesus saw in himself the culmination of

Israel's longings for salvation in God. With the activity of Jesus the time of salvation has begun. God is speaking for the last time. It is significant that Michael Goulder is prepared to admit that the fact that Jesus saw himself as Messiah is the only logical way to account for the ministry of Jesus.[3]

In many ways like this, Jesus transcends the dimensions of manhood and leaves us, as he did his contemporaries, searching for words to describe him and his striking strangeness.

The contention of some scholars today is that we do not need to go outside Jesus locatable in his own time to explain him. This is strongly emphasized in *The Myth of God Incarnate*; that Jesus is quite explicable as a man.

If this is so, it is difficult to understand the extravagant confessional language used by the writers. Michael Goulder speaks of him as the 'man of universal destiny' and others use equally fulsome words of him. John Hick says of him, 'I see the Nazarene, then, as *intensely* and *overwhelmingly* conscious of the reality of God . . . so *powerfully* God conscious that his life vibrated, as it were, to the divine life; and . . . as a result his hands could heal the sick'.[4] 'He was the *most wonderful* man who ever lived'.[5] Jesus is central for *all* that concerns man's relationship with God and *everything* that hangs thereon'[6] (italics mine). Such language clashes with the intention of the book to put everything on an observable, historical basis. In the final chapter of the book, Dennis Nineham, an iconoclast of some standing, is clearly uncomfortable with such descriptions and points out that once you deny the uniqueness of Jesus in his nature the status of such claims becomes impossible to verify; indeed, once one has admitted that Jesus was only human something similar to a 'coach and horses' is run through such ascriptions of power and wonder.

If Jesus is man, and a man of destiny he could well be, why should he, of all people, be a more moral example or a more important redeeming archetype than Moses, Socrates, Buddha or Martin Luther King? Christians brought up within the Christian tradition could possibly understand Jesus as perfect man, but it is hardly compelling to post-christian atheists. Michael Goulder gets himself into some difficulty with this point when over against Muhammad and Gautama Buddha, who are men of universal destiny, he states that 'Jesus is *the* man of universal destiny' (italics his). No reason is given save that Jesus must have seen himself so to be in the prophecy about the Son of man in the book of Daniel.[7] And to say with Hick that 'Jesus was totally and overwhelmingly conscious of the reality of God' is reading a great deal into the naked humanity of Jesus. We must treat this as a 'faith-response' of Professor Hick, no more and no less. What is more, it is a romantic conception of Jesus based upon a rationalistic interpretation of the New Testament. He has replaced the sturdy belief possessed by the early Christians that God had become man tangibly and really, with the notion that 'Jesus was the most wonderful man who ever lived'. True; but only a half-truth because it fails to account for the impact Jesus made on people and the impact he still makes today.

a. It fails to explain fully his disciples' understanding of him
Hick rightly points out in an earlier book that the 'original response was made by his disciples to Jesus as a man, though it was a response which soon deepened into religious faith'.[8] This, in many ways, is a curious confession which is at variance with Hick's rejection of Jesus as properly belonging to and coming from God the Father. It is indeed true that the first believers recognized in him not merely that he was a great man, or the most perfect man, but one who incarnated all the hopes and dreams they, as Jews, had located in the coming of God's kingdom. To include Jesus in the context of religious faith meant a complete shattering of their inherited doctrine as well as their experience of God thus far. It started, of course, with his preaching of the

kingdom which dawned with his coming; what is more, he is not only the proclaimer of it; he is its key and its centre (Lk. 17:20,21; 10:16). When one considers this closely, one is led to see how very remarkable such statements are, because from a Jewish perspective, the distance between God and Jesus has been narrowed significantly. If it is God's kingdom and Jesus is its centre, and if his miracles are the signs of the presence of the kingdom, then the disciples must have jumped, logically, to the conclusion that God was amongst them. 'If it is by the finger of God that I cast out demons, then the kingdom of God has come upon you' (Lk. 11:20). A. M. Hunter points out on this verse that Jesus speaks as one who knows himself to be the Reign of God incarnate.[9]

b. It fails to explain the sense of divine purpose in Jesus

If Jesus is approached purely from the human perspective he becomes more enigmatic, not less so. Consider the sense of mission he so undoubtedly had. The Gospels reveal him as under divine constraint. His ministry is dominated by a purpose to fulfil his Father's will. There is no hesitation concerning this, no fumbling or uncertainty; instead, there is clear direction, even when it entails the stark reality of the cross. Now, if Jesus were a man only, however exemplary and charismatic, we would be hard pressed to find a reason for this assurance. Michael Goulder gives his answer as being that Jesus 'felt himself under the divine "must"; his position in history was foretold in scripture'.[10] This is certainly correct but it doesn't take us very far as an explanation. Moses and the prophets also knew themselves to be under the divine 'must' but their ministries do not compare with the purposeful way Jesus walked forward, interpreting the Scriptures not as a servant, nor as a prophet but as a son. He takes over the 'Son of Man' idea found in Daniel, fills it with new content based on the suffering servant of Isaiah 53 and rides into Jerusalem just before the Passover as the Messiah. All this is very, very strange if we view him only as man. It is, however, explicable and plausible if he is God's son and conscious of that fact and his divine mission. A. M. Hunter again declares of this sense of purpose which separates Jesus from others, 'Search Jewish literature and you will look in vain for a man who prefaces his words with "Amen, I say unto you", who dares to address God as Abba, who tells his disciples that he alone knows the Almighty as Father'.[11]

c. It fails to explain the meaning of God's love

In *The Myth of God Incarnate* God's *agape* (love) in Jesus is mentioned again and again as the *raison d'etre* of Christianity. 'It is supremely through Jesus that the self-giving love of God is most fully expressed and men caught up into the fullest response to him'.[12] 'Jesus not only taught the primacy of *agape*, self-giving love . . . He also founded a community whose keynote it was'.[13] 'We are saved by being incorporated into the society of agape that Jesus founded . . . Jesus' death was, historically, a high probability as the end of his life of self-giving love'.[14] According to Goulder later, Jesus 'was destined by God to establish the community of selfless love in the world'.[15]

Such expressions of faith are grand and, of course, accepted by all Christians. However, we must add two things. First, the word *agape* occurs only five times in Mark, the earliest Gospel, and there are only a few more references in the other synoptic Gospels. It is clear then that *agape* as such does not figure greatly on the lips of Jesus as seen by the synoptic writers even though his whole ministry may be viewed as an aspect of God's love. *Agape* is more frequent in John and Paul, whose conclusions about Christ are treated with some suspicion by the symposium. Now, the point I am making is that these writers are reading back into the synoptic material an idealization of Jesus' message drawn from their own understanding of Christianity. But where are the other aspects which give the love of God in Christ its urgency and strength, such as God's holiness, and the lostness of man? We look for them in vain in *The Myth of God Incarnate*. Secondly, we need to know how, through Jesus, God's self-giving love is expressed when God himself is not personally involved in the action of Jesus. We acknowledge that God identifies with the experiences of all his people, but Maurice Wiles means more than that in the first quotation above. Even if Jesus is God's chosen man, the most perfect man of all times, fully open to God's call, it is hard to understand how he can express God's self-giving love. But if, on the other hand, he is God's incarnate Son, then I can understand it and it makes sense. If Jesus is God's Son and he died for us on the cross, then I can say with Paul 'in Christ God was reconciling the world to himself' (2 Cor. 5:19). Only if there is what is called an ontological relationship, a relationship of nature, between the Father and Jesus can we go on to talk about God's self-giving love in Christ. But if Jesus does not come from God's side to the human family, a divorce is made between God and his world which even a perfect man cannot repair.

Jesus was a man. We all share this starting-point. But I have tried to show that if we restrict Jesus to this plane, his significance cannot fully be seen and his story becomes incoherent. Jesus is man of universal destiny, only if he unites the spheres of deity and humanity in himself. Mythological? We must run the risk of it being called that. But this is not only a modern accusation. During the excavation of the Palatine Palace at Rome, there was discovered a rough drawing of a man worshipping a figure on a cross. The figure has the head of an ass. The graffiti mocks some unknown Christian page perhaps, 'Alexamenos worships God!' While we must try to make our gospel meaningful to modern man we should never forget that the idea of a crucified God has often been an offence to the proud and a scandal to the religious and foolishness to the 'wise'.

3
Who Thought of It First?

We saw in the last chapter that Jesus was believed from the very beginning to be a man, but that in many different ways he confounded people's estimates of him. His *life-style* was different, almost monastic at times, but he did not belong to the Essenes or any other 'way out' sect. Like others he taught, and the content of his teaching can be paralleled in certain respects from rabbinic literature, but he was not a rabbi. His exorcisms and healing miracles can be paralleled from contemporary literature, but he was no mere miracle-worker. Add to this the note of authority to which we referred in the last chapter and we are left with a man who 'did not fit' in his own day.

Was this sufficient reason, then, for his contemporaries to call him divine, the Son of God? No; not on its own. Let's not fall into the trap of assuming that the ancient world was taken in by unusual happenings. The Jews with their fierce monotheism did not go in for calling a human being 'god'. The Greeks might go in for that sort of thing but not they. God was separate from human existence. Although he intervened in human affairs through the offices of angels, his Word and his Spirit, the idea of ascribing divinity to a human being was the highest blasphemy for a few. It is certainly true that they looked for the coming of God's Messiah who would usher in the kingdom, but opinion was divided over the nature of the Messiah and his kingdom. There were those in the first century who believed the Messiah would be someone sent from God, whilst others just as firmly considered that he would arise from among men. Christianity presented two 'scandals' to the Jews; the blasphemy that Jesus was in some form 'God' and that he was crucified (1 Cor. 1:23). We should also remember that whilst 'divine' beings who came to earth were familiar elements in Greek mythology, the Greeks were not taken in easily by claims to divinity; religion was for them a sport, an intellectual equivalent of the 'games'. Jesus with his pedigree would not even make it to the starting-line!

What I am saying is that it is a mistake to believe that people of the first century were gullible and happy to 'divinize' unusual men. This, in fact, is not the case at all.

So then, we are still left with the question, 'Why Jesus?' Was divinity superimposed upon him by the early church or was it integral to his person? Who thought of it first, Jesus or his followers?

Clearly it starts with Jesus. We have already supplied some of the raw data in the previous chapter but there is more we should consider. We shall put to one side for the moment the self-disclosure of Jesus in John's Gospel and concentrate upon the testimony of the other three Gospels.

John is sometimes accused of emphasizing the divinity of Jesus out of proportion to the other Gospel writers. It is in John that we find 'I and the Father are one', and 'before Abraham was, I am', for instance. The grounds for believing these statements to be genuine are just as strong as those which dismiss them as spurious (see page 33ff). The omission of the material from John here is not an admission of its lack of genuineness. It is merely to show that, even without John's assistance, the other Gospel writers were clear that Jesus believed himself divine.

a. Abba (Father)

If we ask 'What aspects identify relationships between persons?' part of the answer would lie in the familiar, intimate language used between people who are close. The closer people are, the more tender and personal becomes the language. So it was with Jesus' relationship to God. It is remarkable that the unanimous testimony of the Gospels is that Jesus used 'Father' in all his prayers (the only exception being Mark 15:34 on the cross). 'It is quite unusual that Jesus should have addressed God as "My Father", it is even more so that he should have used the Aramaic form "Abba" says Prof. J. Jeremias.[1] Why? Simply because 'Abba' was an intimate form of address similar to our word 'Daddy', without the sloppy overtones our title has acquired. Jeremias has drawn attention to the rarity of this word as applied to God. God is rarely addressed as Father in the Old Testament and there are only a few examples of it in Palestinian Judaism during the early Christian era. The personal form 'my Father' is even more exceptional. The first time this appears within Judaism is some time in the Middle Ages! So Jesus' practice of speaking of God as 'Abba' is of fundamental importance to our understanding of him. Jews of his day would have considered it most improper, indeed scandalous, for a man to use such intimate titles for God. Clearly, at this point where Jesus speaks of God as 'my Abba' (Mk. 14:36) we are at the heart of Jesus' relationship to God. He speaks to God as a child does to its father, expressing his trust and obedience to the Father's will in the context of a relationship which transcends all others. Jesus unfailingly spoke of God as 'my Father' and 'your Father' but never as 'our Father'. The impact this address made upon the early church is seen in Paul's twice-mentioned statement that the cry 'Abba! Father!' is the basis of the Christian life and prayer (Rom. 8:15; Gal. 4:6). We have the privilege of calling God 'Abba' through Jesus his Son and through him alone. Because he is Saviour and Lord we share his Sonship in an adoptive, but nevertheless real way.

But when did Jesus begin to be conscious of his unique relationship as Son of the Father? Was he always aware of that relationship? We fully accept that Jesus grew in knowledge and wisdom (Lk. 2:41ff.). Is his own self-awareness part of that also? I see it as a growing thing, similar to our own growth as persons, from babyhood, which includes self-awareness and personhood. So Jesus in obedience, under the hand of his Father, grows under the restraints of his humanity to understand the wonder and implications of his Sonship. Luke 2:41ff. suggests that this self-consciousness which is the other side of his God-consciousness, was fully formed about the time of his becoming 'Bar Mitzvah' (Son of the law) at about the age of twelve. This passage is regarded by some scholars as more a reflection by Luke rather than an actual historical account. We must refrain from so dogmatic a judgment because it is by no means out of place or unlikely that at about that time in his physical growth Jesus showed the first signs of a filial consciousness.

b. Son

As we have already observed, Jesus was extremely reticent concerning self-claims. He did not go bragging about who he was because the character of his mission was such that necessitated a gradual unfolding of his person and work together. Yet to those with eyes to see and a willingness to learn the evidence was before them. He showed God-like power to forgive sins (Lk. 7:48). He asserted his authority over the Temple (Mt. 12:6), the Sabbath (Mt. 12:8), and over Satan's kingdom (Mt. 12:24ff). Some of his direct statements, that would seem preposterous on anyone else's lips, place him without doubt on God's side. He calls men to serve and sacrifice for his sake (Mk. 13:9) and to confess his name is to be blessed by him and accepted by his Father in heaven (Mt. 10:32). He identified the word and will of God with his own (Mt. 7:21–29; Lk. 7:46ff). His use of the expression 'Truly I say to you' was a deliberate substitute for the prophetic 'Thus says the Lord'. We concede that the Son of God should be incognito to all save those with the eyes of faith, but it is impossible to conceive that he was incognito to himself. His ministry just would not make sense.

Three passages in the synoptic Gospels merit special consideration as showing Jesus' understanding of himself as 'Son'.

The first is the baptism of Jesus where he is addressed by God in the words 'Thou art my beloved Son' (Mk. 1:11). Many scholarly attempts have been made to account for the directness of the passage. It seems puzzling to find such a forthright statement before the secrecy which surrounds Jesus' later testimony regarding himself. Some scholars, therefore, suggest that the word was originally 'servant', and that in the post-resurrection development of the Gospel 'servant' was replaced by 'son'. But this is an argument from silence and hardly compelling. Other scholars, on the basis that the background text is Psalm 2:7, suggest that 'son' should be interpreted as Messiah. But, as I. Howard Marshall points out, 'the line of thought appears to be that Jesus is the Messiah because he is the Son of God rather than vice-versa'.[2] That is, Sonship and not Messiahship is the primary reference in the divine utterance. In the passages following the temptations the deeds of Jesus are not associated with messianic expectations but with the presence of God (Mk. 1:24; 2:7).

Secondly, Mark 12:6 gives to Jesus a remarkable role in the purposes of God. In this parable of the vineyard his ministry is seen as being in continuity with that of the prophets of the Old Testament but his relationship to God is quite different. The prophets are 'servants'; he is the 'beloved son' (verse 6). The genuineness of this passage has also been questioned. The explicit reference to 'son', as well as to the death of the son as part of the inevitability of salvation, is said by some to be a creation of the later church. But this argument is not convincing. Given that Jesus, on more than one occasion, referred to his death and was conscious of it as being part of his mission (Mk. 8:31; 10:32) and that he was also conscious of being in a special relationship to God, there is no need to regard the details of the parable with suspicion. Indeed, the story is typical of Jesus' narratives with its build-up and tragic climax. Furthermore, far from the 'son' figure being a later addition, it is integral to the whole. As it stands, the parable is an important part of the New Testament's witness concerning Jesus' awareness of his nature.

The third passage, Matthew 11:27, is the most important of the three. 'All things have been delivered to me by my Father; and no one knows the Son except the Father, and no one knows the Father except the Son and any one to whom the Son chooses to reveal him.' The statement is unusual for two reasons. First, it claims that Jesus possessed a knowledge of God that no one else had. Secondly, that Jesus claimed a Sonship that no one else shared. For a long time scholars have regarded this verse with much suspicion. It seemed too Greek to be authentic on the lips of the carpenter from Nazareth; indeed, it was reminiscent of John's Gospel, and the saying became known as the 'Johannine thunderbolt'. But of late, the force of this view has weakened considerably, because research has shown that, rather than being a Greek saying, it is clearly Jewish in style. The importance of this is obvious. If this passage is rejected it can no longer be on the grounds that it is Greek and later, but on the grounds of one's general approach to Jesus himself. There is, in other words, no sufficient reason for rejecting it as a real statement uttered by Jesus.

In this passage, remarkable because it is another of those rare, explicit self-disclosures by Jesus, we are confronted with a statement of a unique relationship between Jesus and his Father. While it does not express the meaning of Sonship in all its fullness, it is explicit enough and would have seemed to Jewish ears a most outrageous claim. 'My Father and I', Jesus is asserting, 'know one another intimately and this relationship is exclusive. Because of this personal knowledge I reveal the Father to those who link their lives with mine.' It was statements like this which were at the heart of the offence of Jesus and which drove him to the cross.

c. His resurrection

Hans Küng writes that the central puzzle of Jesus' life is 'How did this condemned heretical teacher become Israel's Messiah, the Christ? How did this disowned prophet become "Lord", how did this unmasked seducer of the people become "Saviour", this rejected blasphemer "God's son"?'[3]

If there is one single fact we must claim to be decisive for the divinity of Jesus it is surely the resurrection. Anyone can make statements about being God; many have lived exemplary lives; some have taught beautiful things; a few have done miracles; but Jesus' resurrection puts him in a special category. Now, in the space of a small book there is no room to consider the evidence for the resurrection. Readers should refer to George Ladd's recent book *I believe in the resurrection of Jesus Christ*[4] or Michael Green's *Man Alive!*[5] for balanced and stimulating treatments of the historicity of this great event. But with the resurrection of Jesus, the story of Jesus enters a new stage. From this point on Jesus the Proclaimer becomes Jesus the Proclaimed. He who spoke about God's kingdom which was veiled and ambiguous in his person, is now seen in his resurrection as its first-fruit. Jesus in his teaching turned his listeners' attention to the universal resurrection of the dead, God's judgment upon all men, and the necessity for all to enter the kingdom as 'little children'. Jesus' own resurrection was, therefore, clearly seen as a foretaste of these great events. The last days have now dawned.

The significance of the resurrection for the disciples' understanding of Jesus cannot be overstated. It meant, for a start, that the earthly ministry of Jesus was confirmed. His claims to authority which amounted to putting himself in God's place, so blasphemous to the Jew, were now vindicated. So Peter in his opening sermon in Acts accuses the Jews of murdering an innocent man; he was unjustly put to death (Acts 2:23). Peter cannot and does not deny that Jesus was condemned partly on the grounds of blasphemy, but the point is that the resurrection proves that that was a false charge. 'God has made him both Lord and Christ, this Jesus whom you crucified' (Acts 2:36). We must not interpret this as saying that the resurrection has raised Jesus to the heights of divinity. Peter is not saying that the human person Jesus was adopted by God but simply stating that the resurrection attests the authority of Jesus, that he is Saviour and he is God's way of salvation. Through God's mighty act of raising Jesus the veil covering his glory has been removed. He is Lord and Christ.

But the resurrection means, secondly, that if Jesus has been raised from the dead, then God is revealed in Jesus. If the resurrection displays God's victory over sin and death then obviously God himself is personally involved in this action. We cannot separate the work of God the Father from that of Jesus. To interpret this event as though Jesus is God's means of achieving his ends as his human representative, is to drive a wedge between them both. On the contrary, if the resurrection is the climax of God's work of salvation; if the end-time has begun in this amazing act, then God's raising of Jesus testifies to the Sonship of Jesus. The early church arrived logically at this conclusion. The resurrection brought all the elements together. Like a key piece in a jig-saw puzzle it makes sense of all the other pieces and so completes the picture. This is partly why I find it extraordinary that John Hick can quote George Caird with approval: 'Let us suppose that tomorrow you were confronted with irrefutable evidence that an acquaintance whom you had good reason to believe dead had been seen alive by reliable witnesses. You would certainly feel compelled to revise some of your ideas about science, but I doubt whether you would feel compelled to revise your ideas about God. I doubt whether you would conclude that your acquaintance was divine or that a stamp of authenticity had been placed on all he ever said or did'.[6] But there is an error of logic here because a crucial piece of data has been omitted. In the case of such an unlikely event as a friend arising from the grave, it is true that we would not jump automatically to the conclusion that he was divine. But we are not talking about a 'Tom, Dick or Harry' who rises, but one who spoke about rising, whose entire ministry was dominated by the events of death and resurrection. Surely, with the resurrection of such a one we would be compelled to revise our opinion of God. In other words, the resurrection of John Hick's man is discontinuous with that man's life; it is a surprise, without preparation or explanation, but with Jesus the resurrection rounds off his ministry.

The resurrection, then, represents the climax of Jesus' life and ministry and interprets all he stood for. Kierkegaard once said that 'life must be lived forwards but understood backwards'. This is true as we seek to understand our own existence under God's guidance; it was also true of Jesus. The resurrection did not supply the early church with a strange new piece of data to add to the enigma of their master but it was the 'coping-stone' which now made sense of him. In so being, it became not only the triumphant final curtain upon the earthly ministry of the Lord but also a fresh point of departure for the church. Now in plumbing the depths of Jesus' being the Christians discovered they were plumbing the very heart of God, as well as that of man.

4
How Much Did the Early Church Invent?

It is often claimed that the church made Jesus divine. Paul, especially, is singled out as the villain of the piece as the one who diverted the course of Christianity by ignoring the human Jesus and fantasizing his own ideas of faith. This is, of course, a serious accusation sharpened by the fact that it is constantly repeated. The impression is thus given that the churches of the primitive period invented their own glorified pictures of Jesus which bore little resemblance to the real man.

The question we need to ask then is this, 'Is it true that Paul, John and other New Testament writers seriously distorted, however innocently, the figure and significance of Jesus?' If they did, then the whole course of Christianity is suspect and Christian theology is built upon sand. The search for the real Christ becomes an urgent necessity if the New Testament got it wrong. Did they?

Everyone agrees that the New Testament does not set out to give a biography of Jesus or detached treatises on 'The Nature of Faith'. Of course not. It stems not from the study but from the living situation of Christians, in prison, in debate and argument, in pastoral care of churches and individuals. The New Testament is, in other words, applied literature. Little of it is carefully worked out theology. Paul's letter to the Romans *might* be the exception. All of it assumes one simple fact; that Jesus is Lord. It is, thus, an interpretation of Jesus. It is not history, although history is important for Christians who believe that Jesus is a historical figure; neither is it biography, although Christians are interested in Jesus who lived and ministered in Galilee. The New Testament is a testimony to Jesus Christ. In fact, when one looks at the writings which make up the New Testament, their emphasis on the central figure of Christ is very remarkable. It is best summed up in Professor C. F. D. Moule's comment on Paul's staggering description of Christ as the fullness of the Godhead, quoted on page 5 'the identification of that historical person – the Nazarene so ignominiously executed – with the subject of this description is staggering, and fairly cries out for some explanation'.[1]

But before we can think of explanations there are two fundamental questions we need to answer:

a. What did Paul and the other apostles know of the historic Jesus?
Actually quite a bit, contrary to what we are sometimes given to believe! They knew he was a Jew (Gal. 4:4); he had brothers (Gal. 1:19; 1 Cor. 9:5); he was poor (2 Cor. 8:9); he knew temptation and hardship (Heb. 5:8); he was obedient (Heb. 3:2). They also knew sayings of the Lord and were clearly aware of his teaching (1 Cor. 7:10 etc; Rom. 12:19–21). In other words, the impression given is that they proceeded from the assumption of the full humanity of Jesus.

b. What connection did Paul and the apostles have with the Jewish community in Jerusalem?
The hypothesis that Paul invented the Christ of faith is based on the presupposition that Paul's links with the Jerusalem community were loose in the extreme and that he

was regarded by them as a suspicious character. But this is far from the case. While Paul's ministry in Asia was vexed by some 'Judaizers' who questioned his apostleship and denied his teaching, there is not the slightest evidence that his gospel differed in any major way from that of the other apostles (Gal. 1:22–24). Peter and Paul may once have been at loggerheads over some matters of Christian behaviour but there was no difference over fundamental matters of faith. That is the reason why Paul could charge Peter with inconsistency; they shared the same belief in the gospel of grace. While Paul insists on the divine origin of his apostolic commissioning, he is careful nevertheless to point out that it received the confirmation and approval of the Jerusalem church (Gal. 2:1–2). Elsewhere in Paul's writings the importance of the 'tradition' (*paradosis*) received by him from the church is stressed; for example, about worship (1 Cor. 11:2), the Last Supper (1 Cor. 11:23), and about Jesus' death and resurrection (1 Cor. 15:3). Furthermore, it is now widely recognized that Paul's theology and ideas, far from being Greek in origin, are solidly based on Jewish thinking. We do not have to look outside Judaism to explain Paul's terminology and framework of ideas. We must, of course, go outside Judaism to explain the content of Paul's theology, and that is to Christ himself.

Let us look at the character of Christ as seen by these writers.

The first thing we notice is that Jesus is a risen Christ. This, as we have seen, is the corner-stone of Christianity. It is there in every stratum of the New Testament. – It is implied in Hebrews, quite explicit in the Gospels, Acts and John's writings, but nowhere more central than in Paul's letters. The resurrection, to Paul, was the key to understanding Christ as well as the Christian life. Paul's testimony was simply that it was the risen Christ who met him on the Damascus road and transformed his way of looking at religion and life: 'For it is God who said, "Let light shine out of darkness," who has shone in our hearts to give the light of the knowledge of the glory of God in the face of Christ' (2 Cor. 4:6).

Secondly, the risen Christ is Lord. While, indeed, Jesus was always Lord, the application of the term after the resurrection is appropriate since it declares his Lordship and makes it effective (Rom. 1:4). 'Jesus is Lord' was most probably the earliest Christian confession and was used in baptismal ceremonies as well as before pagan magistrates who demanded allegiance to Caesar as 'lord'. The early Christians must have seemed not only a stubborn lot but an odd lot as well. There was considerable latitude about religious practices in the ancient world, and people were not persecuted for belief as long as they adopted a 'live and let live' philosophy. The Christians did not toe the line. For a start they refused to recognize other gods and secondly they applied the title 'lord' exclusively to Jesus. No wonder they were called *'atheoi'* (atheists!) because they called into question the 'multi-religious' philosophy and policy of the mighty Roman Empire. Persecution was inevitable. As for the origin of the term, we do not have to go outside Judaism to find the explanation. The title 'Lord' was regularly used of Yahweh. On the basis of Scripture, therefore, the title was applied to Jesus by the primitive church long before Paul appeared on the scene. We find it used in the early preaching (Acts 2:21; 9:15,21; 22:16) and it is used in the cry 'Marana tha!' (Our Lord, come!) (1 Cor. 16:22).

Thirdly, the risen Lord Christ is worshipped. Christian theology is confession shaped by a unique form, that is, worship. It is not, as we have already observed, fashioned in a detached manner but in the context of response to One who meets us as the risen Lord and Saviour. For Paul, Christ is someone worshipped alongside God the Father and with the Spirit (1 Cor. 1:2). For John, the true response of the believer is to join in Thomas's confession 'My Lord and my God!' (Jn. 20:28). For the writer of the Hebrews also, Christ is worthy of worship because, unlike the angels and created beings, he shares the divine nature (Heb. 1:5).

Finally, the risen Lord is in some way 'God'. It is important to point out that the New Testament is aware of the implications involved in ascribing divinity to Jesus. As Jews, the writers must have been conscious of separating from Jewish tradition at this point, but no other option was open to them. Not for them the careful circumlocution of some modern theologians who mince around the scandal saying that 'Jesus embodies the way of God towards men'. In their view the evidence demanded the conclusion that Jesus shared the divine nature and could be measured by no other standard than God himself. While, indeed, they all took over the messianism of the synoptics as the starting-point for understanding Jesus, they could not see this as in any adequate way explaining the full significance of Jesus. We shall see in a moment how some of them interpreted Jesus in the light of their own situation, but it was the fact and the meaning of the resurrection which above all else drove them remorselessly to the opinion that Jesus in a special and unique way shared the very nature of God. No other conclusion fitted the facts of his person and work. In responding to Jesus men were responding to God. This is how it seemed to them. Not only did this involve them in clarifying what they believed about Christ but led to a fresh understanding of God himself.

We can now see how in the development of understanding concerning Jesus, the earliest statements concerning 'this man Jesus' (Acts 2:36) were soon to develop into more depth and detail. Once it was recognized that Jesus was divine and that his mission was God's mission the notion of pre-existence inevitably entered into the teaching of the church.

Let us now glance at the contribution of three of the most important New Testament writers to discover their understanding of Jesus.

Paul
When comparisons are made between the synoptic Gospels and Paul's writings, usually to Paul's disadvantage, it is often

forgotten that Paul's letters are among the earliest in the New Testament and were written in the course of his ministry, AD *c*.47–*c*.66, close to the events of Jesus' life. When this is borne in mind, together with the very high view of Christ which Paul has, we have a very impressive testimony to the impact Jesus made upon people. But Paul's interest is not in the human Jesus but in the risen Christ. He states, 'even though we once regarded Christ from a human point of view, we regard him thus no longer. Therefore, if any one is in Christ, he is a new creation; the old has passed away, behold, the new has come' (2 Cor. 5:16,17). The background of 2 Corinthians was that Paul had been reproached for not having had personal connections with Christ and for consequently being inferior to those who had known the human Jesus. Paul's reply is that in the light of the resurrection, personal relations are out of date in the face of the wonderful newness in Christ. It matters little whether one has known the human Jesus personally or not, for even those who knew him in that tangible human body no longer know him in that way now. Christ's mortal life counts for nothing. The thing that matters is that, since his resurrection, Christ has changed the world and made all things new for the believer.

We cannot avoid the fact that Paul's view of Christ is 'from above' (see page 39). He does not dwell upon the question at what point did the incarnation begin, but he does not shrink from declaring boldly that in the human Jesus God has chosen the way to make himself known by becoming man. It is very hard to understand, then, how a scholar can assert that the 'notion of God being incarnate in the traditionally accepted sense is read into, not out of, the Pauline epistles',[2] because the idea that God has taken upon himself humanity is so obviously there in Paul's thought. A few passages will be sufficient to illustrate this point.

1. *Galatians 4:4,5*; 'But when the time had fully come, God

sent forth his Son, born of woman, born under the law'. Here, the intention is to underline the abasement of the Son in his mission. Christ is put under the law, in order to redeem those who are in bondage to it, so as to make them sons of God. A similar idea is repeated in Romans 8:3. 'Sending his own Son in the likeness of sinful flesh and for sin, he condemned sin in the flesh.' We are saved, Paul asserts, by Christ's act of taking our nature upon him. Here, similarity and difference play important roles in the argument. Christ takes human nature yet he is without sin. Quite obviously, this was a crucial element in Paul's thought because it is echoed yet again in 2 Corinthians 5:21, 'He made him to be sin who knew no sin'. In this aspect of sinlessness, together with the 'sending of the Son' mentioned in the two previous verses, there are strong allusions to the pre-existence of the Son. Christ was always Son of God but in becoming man he did not surrender his unique nature. There is no way of avoiding the uncompromising language of such passages.

2. *Philippians 2:5-11.* This great hymn to Christ lays bare the rich depths of Paul's thought. If, as many scholars believe, the passage was a hymn current in the church the significance of the passage is greater; it reveals widespread belief in the incarnation. But as it is integral to Paul's argument in the passage we shall treat it as revealing Paul's understanding of his Lord's voluntary humiliation which becomes deeper and deeper as he enters into human experience. The stages are plain enough: his humility with reference to the Godhead, his obedience as a son, his abasement as a servant, even to the point of death. This is the reason for his exaltation and for the privileges of exercising a dominion over all, which are now doubly his. It may be helpful to put this in terms of a schematization showing four steps down from glory to the degradation of abasement, and the four steps up to a glory now seen by the whole of creation.

Steps to humiliation	Steps to glory
(v.6) Denied himself	Universal confession (v.11)
(v.7) Emptied himself	Universal worship (v.10)
(v.8) Humbled himself	Greatest name (v.9)
(v.8) Obedient to death	Highest exaltation (v.9)

Paul's concern here is not on the metaphysics of the incarnation. The question *how* a divine being can become man is not a question that bothers him; his interest, rather, is upon the humiliation of Christ in his human life. Whereas to the original disciples the astounding paradox must have been that the man whose companions they had been, and who died so shamefully, was now acclaimed as Lord, to Paul the astounding paradox was that such an exalted One should become man and die. Although he took human nature, and we must remember that Paul did not believe Jesus was a phantom but a *real* person, Christ was from everlasting the Son of God, yet he came among us stripped of his glory and dignity. Though he shared the divine nature and privileges, in love for men he chose the way of incarnation. What did he empty himself of? Certainly not his divine nature; the passage gives us no grounds for assuming that, but rather he emptied himself of those marks of status which were his by right.

Space does not allow us to consider other equally important passages. A glance, however, at 2 Corinthians 8:9; Colossians 1:18–25 and Ephesians 1:3–10 will show that Paul's view of Christ dominated his entire theology and interpreted his whole attitude to life and creation, to death and beyond. His ministry, and personal goal he sums up simply in Philippians 3:10 'That I may know him and the power of his resurrection, and may share his sufferings, becoming like him in his death'.

John

John is the profoundest New Testament interpreter of Christ's person. The purpose of the Gospel is declared boldly in John 20:31. 'These (things) are written that you may believe that Jesus is the Christ, the Son of God, and that believing you may have life in his name.' If we had to reduce the message of the Gospel to one sentence it might be something like this: Jesus Christ is the only way of salvation because the Father is personally present in the Son and the Son in the Father.

John's Gospel is, of course, quite different from the synoptics probably because his concerns are different. While it is apparent that he knew the synoptic material, he did not draw upon that tradition but upon independent sources which supplemented the rest. Over the years John's Gospel has had a bad press. Its historical reporting has been questioned and its reliability as a commentary on the teaching of Jesus has also been suspected. There is no need to adopt such a negative and critical line. Just because a witness has a different perspective on things from other witnesses it does not follow either that he is wrong or that contradictions abound. Over recent years a more positive role has been given to the Fourth Gospel and a higher regard paid to the slants it gives. So, for example, it is widely recognized that much of John's traditions go back to pre-AD 70 Palestine and are not inferior to the synoptic tradition. Archaeology has vindicated some of John's place names and the topography of Jerusalem as shown in the Gospel.[3]

But how should we respond to Goulder's charge that 'the full work of divinizing Jesus falls to John, who has no mere human being but the Word of God incarnated, striding an inch above the ground'?[4] What Goulder is implying is that John's view of Christ is false because it is different from the other Gospels, and, we might add, different from Goulder's own conclusions! As we have already mentioned John's view of Christ is different, and the difference amounts to this, that in John there is no veiling of Christ's person. Christ is there for all to see as Son of God and Saviour. The Gospel sets out to show that Jesus was the unique Son of God (chapter 1) and in the development of Jesus' ministry his superiority over all and his universal significance are set forth.

Drawing upon different terms and titles John shows the special character of Jesus. Logos, Rabbi, Messiah, the Coming One, Prophet, King of Israel, and Son of God; all these terms are applied to him and pay homage to him culminating in the supreme pronouncement made by Thomas, 'My Lord and my God!'

Two points can be made at once on the different picture of Christ that John portrays. First, there is no need to go beyond the Old Testament to understand the meaning of the terms or their significance. They are saying simply, yet boldly, that one should address Jesus in the same ways in which the Jew addressed Yahweh. Secondly, John is not portraying a 'docetic' Jesus, that is, a Jesus who only *appeared* to be human. The humanity of Jesus is obviously there in John (Jn. 1:4; 4:6) as well as in the Epistles which bear his name and stamp (2 Jn. 7). While Jesus is bold concerning his identity, the scandal of Jesus comes out as strongly as it does in the other Gospels; as far as his enemies and uninterested bystanders are concerned nothing extra-ordinary distinguished him from other men (Jn. 7:40–44). Only those with the eyes of faith could really appreciate that God was among them (Jn. 6:66–69).

Perhaps the greatest legacy John has left the Christian church is his teaching about Jesus as the Logos. 'In the beginning was the *Logos*, and the *Logos* was with God, and the *Logos* was God' (Jn. 1:1) so the Prologue begins, reaching its soaring climax in 'No one has ever seen God; the only Son, who is in the bosom of the Father, he has made him known' (v.18). There is no mistaking the incarnation doctrine here. Here is an invasion of humanity by God who becomes 'flesh' and dwells among us (v.14). It does not say, we should note, that the Word 'entered' flesh, or 'abided' in flesh but *became* flesh. Whereas the ancient Greeks yearned for release from the flesh, God takes it fully upon himself. The Epistles of John are even more anxious to establish the humanity of Jesus over against those who asserted that the divine being only 'seemed' to be human. 'Every spirit which confesses that Jesus Christ has come in the flesh is of God, and every spirit which does not confess Jesus is not of God' (1 Jn. 4:2).

When John declares that the 'Word became flesh and dwelt among us' we are being told that in Jesus we have the localization of God's presence upon earth. Indeed, he now replaces the ancient Tabernacle which housed the 'Shekinah' glory of God.

Hebrews

A third great interpreter of Jesus is the unknown writer of the letter to the Hebrews which was probably written about AD 62–66 to a Jewish Christian community in Rome. By the look of things these people were losing heart because of the difficulties associated with being Christians and they looked wistfully back to the attractions of Judaism. The writer exhorts them to remain firm and he reminds them of the superiority of Christianity. Above all else, he concentrates upon Jesus as exemplifying the greatness of Christianity. Using categories they will understand and going to the heart of their problem the writer shows how Christ fulfills all the demands of the Jewish sacrificial system as priest and victim. He is a greater high priest than Aaron and the priests of the Old Covenant because he abides for ever and because his sacrifice is complete and unrepeatable (Heb. 6:20; 7:27) it does not need continual repetition; it is final.

But what is the ground for this assertion? Simply this, that Jesus is God's Son in a unique fashion, superior to men, angels and all created things. Indeed, he is creator and preserver (Heb. 1:2,3) and reflects the 'effulgence' of God's glory.

Like John and Paul, this writer has a doctrine of the incarnation. Although he is Son and shares the glory of God the Father, he is made a little lower than the angels in a temporary yet real humiliation; *real* because the writer stresses the humanity of Jesus in the weakness of his flesh. This aspect is very important for the writer because one of his concerns is to show that Jesus was tempted in all points as we are, yet without sin. It was a real manhood, authentic and unimpaired and, as such, an indispensable qualification for his office as priest because he can intercede for sinners. But it is a *temporary* humiliation also. He did not begin to be from the moment of his earthly ministry but is the eternal Son of God; as Son he sits at God's right hand (Heb. 1:3) and watches over his people (Heb. 7:25; 9:24).

Analysis

In our brief description of three important witnesses we have been aware of the charge that their theologies of Jesus owe more to idealizations created by their Christian communities than to Jesus himself. Are we in a position now to answer this criticism? I believe we are.

First, the position cannot be put baldly that Paul, Hebrews and John represent later development. As we have noted, Paul and Hebrews were probably written before the synoptic Gospels, and John's traditions are early also, and this should be taken into account when one is talking in terms of primary and secondary sources. Their high views of Christ written so soon after the events must be taken into account and not lightly dismissed as later creations.

Secondly, those who try to divide the historical Jesus from the rest of the New Testament often fail to make sufficient allowance for the figure of Jesus. He is 'humanized' by them to such an extent that he becomes as weak and as fallible a creature as an ordinary being. Current New Testament scholarship generally agrees on the greatness of Jesus' personality and ministry in his own time. Instead of a human Jesus in the synoptics, and a glorified, docetic Christ in Paul and John, we have to reckon with a man who was larger than life. His self-awareness and God-consciousness make us aware that the synoptic Gospels have by no means exhausted the significance of Jesus. Rather, they prepare the way for the fuller treatments given by such writers as we have considered.

Thirdly, we should not ignore those elements that writers like Paul, John, and the writer to the Hebrews took over from the earliest disciples closest to Jesus. Christ's complete manhood, his Messiahship and the recognition of him as 'Lord' were taken over from the primitive community and became central elements in their teaching. There is no conflict between them, only development of what had been implicit.

Fourthly, in all three writers, and especially in Paul and John, the resurrection is decisive for their understanding of Jesus and is the central motif in their teaching. Just as we might say that the moon and the modern world have not been quite the same since 20 July 1969 when the first human being walked on the surface of the moon, so we can say in a more profound way that the resurrection of Jesus changed men's ways of looking at the world and God. It not only interpreted the past but it gave to the future a new content and richer and more exciting possibilities. In Christ, God's future had dawned. So we can say that the New Testament writers gained new understanding of God himself through Christ, which could only result in giving to Christ applications and values tradition had given to God alone. This is not distortion, but description of one who still calls men to confess him as Lord.

5
Who Died: Why?

A friend of mine once spoke to a group of scientists about the meaning of Christianity. After he finished a man arose and asked, 'But what on earth is the relevance to us today of the death of a man, however good, who died nearly two thousand years ago?' My friend replied, 'If it were the death of a good man, I would agree with you that the relevance would be slight. But if that death were in some way God's, then it has all the relevance in the world.'

Our theme is the person of Christ, but as we have seen already, the issues involved in discussing Jesus are far from academic. Christianity is a down-to-earth affair; the purpose of the incarnation was not to allow God a spectacular form of astro-travel but to rescue man from the predicament of sin. Indeed, I would go so far as to say with Karl Barth that the cross is the real centre of the Christian faith; it is at this point in Jesus' career that the purpose of Christ is discovered. So Kahler exclaims, 'without the Cross there is no Christology nor is there any feature in Christology which can escape justifying itself by the Cross'. [1]

But what a strange place to find God incarnate, at the point of death! Celsus, a pagan intellectual in the third century, poured great scorn on the idea of Christians who worshipped a crucified Saviour.[2] The New Testament gives testimony to the embarrassment the cross created for proud non-Christians (1 Cor. 1:23). But there is no way of avoiding this narrow door; it is the close connection between incarnation and atonement which makes Christianity what it is.

However, like the chicken and egg question, the question 'Is the starting-point of Christian theology the incarnation or the atonement?' is often put. Catholics have tended to concentrate upon the former and Protestants the latter, but unless we hold both together our grasp of New Testment teaching is bound to be deficient. Incarnation does not take place as an end in itself but for the purposes of man's redemption, so that God's eternal and sacrificial love may be revealed and applied. In Christ's action on the cross we have the place where the purpose of his coming is displayed and the veil lifted from his teaching and ministry. The cross becomes the place where God and man face each other; where man as he is faces God as he is.

But can there be salvation without God who is incarnate? Indeed there can be, but the question is, what kind of salvation is it? It is said today that there are basically two types of theories about Christ; one 'from above', the other 'from below'. Those 'from below' begin with Jesus as a man and assume his full and entire manhood, and, generally speaking, resist speaking about God becoming man in the traditional sense. Those 'from above', as in this present essay, while not denying his manhood, view Christ's coming as first and foremost the action of God himself. Let us see, then, how one view 'from below' handles the question. In John Robinson's book, *The Human Face of God*, we have a lucid, and in some ways an admirable and sensitive expression of the view of Christ 'from below'. For Robinson, Jesus was 'totally and utterly a man – and had never been anything other than a man or more than a man'.[3] Yet this Jesus is God's man who dares to stand in the place of God as his representative and to be God for man. Robinson quotes the reformer, Melanchthon, 'to know Christ is to know his benefits',[4] but what benefits does Robinson direct us to? It is to ethical and mystical insights based upon the transparent and awesome life of Jesus who is the human face of God. But salvation, as seen in the biblical sense of God's victory over man's sin and the restoration of man to God, hardly gets a mention at all. In Robinson's view, the supernatural framework used to support God's action in Christ must be abandoned.

A similar view is met with in Michael Goulder's essay in *The Myth of God Incarnate*. His view is less subtle than Robinson's and this has the advantage of being more clearcut. Jesus is also a man of integrity and destiny who lived love and founded his community of love. Goulder also rejects completely traditional theories of Jesus' death, and instead treats it as the inevitable outcome of a loving life. He died a martyr; his death a crown to his life. He probably knew his death was inevitable and so 'By the completeness of his faithfulness unto death Jesus achieved unwittingly the destiny which he had followed all his ministry, the actualization of God's kingdom in a society of love that was permanent'.[5]

Now, a test we must apply to any theological system is that of coherence. While Robinson and Goulder are wholehearted in their rejection of supernatural explanations, the extraordinary respect they give to the man Jesus needs some explanation, as we observed in chapter 2. Why Jesus? Their Jesus, taken out of his New Testament context appears like a leader of a 20th century civil rights movement! An admirable figure indeed, but inexplicable. Furthermore, the purpose of his coming does not make sense either. The stripping away of ideas that modern people find unpalatable leaves Jesus as a more mysterious figure than ever before, and not as compelling. Take this martyr idea. Many people have died for their beliefs as martyrs, and we are normally given data in their statements or actions which suggest that their deaths are completing the logical outworking of their lives. Is this true of Jesus? Indeed not. It is far too narrow a concept to apply to Jesus and it ignores the strange development of his career with its mixture of claims and silences, his deeds and teachings, his identity with God and man. It ignores his strange behaviour of dread at the approaching cross and it ignores the universal belief of the early church that Jesus' death was unique, a sacrifice for sin. An odd thing to say of a martyr! Furthermore, we might add, Jesus, from a human perspective, was not a notably good martyr. Others have died more courageously than he if we ignore the fact that he was facing being made sin for us, such as the young Christian girl Blandina who was roasted alive for her faith at the end of the 2nd century. Unless we see Jesus' dread as involving him in bearing the awful punishment and condemnation for the world's evils, then Jesus' death becomes a less-than-average martyrdom.

When the study of Jesus is approached from the side of man there are some decided advantages which we readily acknowledge. It is a full and recognizable manhood that is being asserted without any problems about a divine nature being added to the human. Jesus is the same as anyone else, differing only according to the excellence of his life and destiny, and the incarnation is but a development of God's involvement with man through the prophets, saints and sages of the Old Testament.

But the disadvantages are great in many respects. We have already mentioned that the coherence of a theology is an important test of its validity.

What we believe about Christ relates to many other doctrines of the Christian faith, to the Trinity, to God the Father, to sin and man's need as well as to salvation. Our understanding of Christ is like the clutch of a car; if it fails to mesh with the gears, then you must replace the clutch, not the whole engine. *Now concerning the Trinity*; if Jesus is approached solely from the perspective of man, then the doctrine of the Trinity as traditionally defined must surely go. How can there be a Trinity if the Second Person is denied? If his pre-existence is rejected, then an eternal trinitarianism becomes impossible to hold; if Jesus becomes part of the Godhead through his obedience as 'God's Man' in what way can we still uphold his equality with the Father and Spirit? *Concerning God the Father*; if Jesus is seen from man's viewpoint, even as God's Man differing only from us by degree, then of necessity he is different in kind from God. The whole point of views 'from below' is that Jesus shares *our* nature and not God's; as such he is recognizable as our brother. However, as we have seen, the New Testament claims for Jesus a unique relationship with the Father that *no one else* shares and that this is the basis of his mission. If this framework is rejected, our understanding of Christ is left in the air because God's involvement in Jesus is tenuous in the extreme and certainly not a personal involvement. To use H. E. W. Turner's phrase, proponents of this view are working with 'one dimension short'.[6] *Concerning sin*; if Jesus comes from the side of man we can say confidently that he shares man's nature, but can we say as clearly and surely as St Paul that 'he knew no sin'? Sin in the Bible is not just a moral thing in the life of the individual, but a state, a disease, which permeates the whole life of man, and influences the whole range of human experiences. However good a man Christ must have been, if he were just a man there is no way he could have escaped the corruption of sin. The testimony of the New Testament is direct on this matter, that Christ, the sinless Son of God, takes *fallen* nature upon himself and out of that unlikely material lives out a life of perfect obedience.

We must grasp the nettle on this last point. The difference between radical restatements of Jesus and traditional theories boils down to the question, 'What are people being saved from?' Traditional notions of sin as constituting an eternal barrier between God and man, which can be removed only by a saviour who can fully represent both parties in the drama, are firmly rejected by such theologians as Cupitt, Wiles, Robinson, Pittenger, Knox and others. The doctrine of the Fall is dismissed along with the idea of original sin. It is replaced by an evolutionary concept in which God works in creation through his appointed saviour who invites sinners to join in the divine activity of redeeming man and God's creation. We must recognize that on this point we have the most serious rift between the two points of view and, as far as can be seen, there is such incompatibility between them that harmonization is impossible. But what is at issue is the nature of salvation and the character of the redeemer. In the one view sin is dark and serious and, if not a constituent part of human nature, at least it influences human nature very profoundly. In the other view, while sin is still a reality it is not seen in the same depth and its moral and spiritual effects not as black. We can only point out these differences and leave the reader to decide 'Which view is supported by the teachings of the Bible? Which fits the facts of human experience and the world as we look within and without?'

I can only affirm that the Bible treats sin as a most serious thing, and man's separation from God as the most tragic fact in creation. The Bible is shot through with the problem of man's alienation from God and man's desperate and pitiful attempts to justify himself. The sacrificial system, the moral teaching of the prophets, the constant failure of Israel, the pleadings of Yahweh for his people to return, John the Baptist's call to repent, the coming of Jesus; all this depicts the plight and folly of man. We look around at our world and we see little evidence that the world is any better, morally, ethically and spiritually than the ancient world from which our Bible comes. Civilization and education have failed to make us better people. What is more, the problem of guilt still remains, with accompanying feelings of moral responsibility for failure, and the desire to find fulfilment. P. T. Forsyth, commenting on man's need, wrote, 'So great is a soul and so great its sin that each man is only saved by an act which at the same time saves the whole world'.[7]

So then, let us look at this saving act in its two aspects of human and divine responses.

Salvation requires a human representative
We have already agreed that the New Testament teaches the humanity of the Lord. The reason for this is expressed very clearly in Hebrews which alone of the New Testament writings is directly concerned with the meaning of the incarnation of the Son of God. The writer argues that 'In the days of his flesh, Jesus offered up prayers and supplications, with loud cries and tears, to him who was able to save him from death, and he was heard for his godly fear. Although he was a Son, he learned obedience through what he suffered; and being made perfect he became the source of eternal salvation to all who obey him' (Heb. 5:7–9). This is surely one of the most remarkable statements in the New Testament concerning the humanity of Jesus. The writer is holding in balance two apparently contradictory viewpoints. On the one hand, Jesus is the Son of the eternal God, heir of all things and possessor of stature above all others. Yet, on the other hand, the eternal Son enters into the experiences of life, grows in obedience and through his sufferings becomes the way to life. The writer sets himself to answer the question, 'Why was it necessary for God to become man?' and he replies in the following way:
1. That he who saves others from bondage must be identified with them in every conceivable way.
2. That he who wishes to restore others to obedience to God must himself know what obedience is.

As for the first point, the writer points out the identification of Jesus with men and their human needs; he knows our weaknesses (Heb. 4:15; 5:2), he was tempted (Heb. 4:15), he knew pain and anguish (Heb. 5:7), he experienced fear (Heb. 5:8), he tasted death for all men (Heb. 2:9). Such identification has only one end; as a means of salvation for others. The human priest chosen by men to act on their behalf does so on the basis of his similarity to sinners. So

Christ enters into the human lot to take upon himself the strains of men's burdens and to offer on their behalf that sacrifice for sin they cannot provide.

Secondly, the note of obedience is seen as an important response for Jesus as a representative to offer. Sin, in the Epistle, has already been described as 'disobedience' (Heb. 2:2; 3:7–12; 3:18). It is a wilful turning away from God. The writer mentions Moses approvingly as someone who was faithful in God's house as a servant (Heb. 3:5), yet Christ as Son demonstrates the faithfulness that should mark all of God's children, especially in respect of obedience to the Father's will. It is more than likely that the writer has in mind the story of the Fall with its central message of disobedience. (See also Phil. 2:5–11 where this is also probable.) While this may be in the background, the point being made by Hebrews is that obedience is an on-going thing through life which in Christ's case culminates in death. Not that the cross was a test of obedience but rather its triumphant conclusion, because obedience to his Father's will took him to the place where, personally, he did not *want* to go, but where he *had* to go to become saviour.

The teaching of Hebrews is an example of the testimony of the New Testament as a whole that, if man was going to be saved from the penalty and pain of sin, only a man could pay it. Jesus goes to his cross with this firm intention: 'A second Adam to the fight and to the rescue came'.

Salvation must be of God
The full grandeur of New Testament Christianity is spelled out in the words that 'in Christ God was reconciling the world to himself' (2 Cor. 5:19). It was not man making initiatives to save, but God who acts in his amazing work of becoming man in Jesus and dying for the human race. The action is that of grace: what man could not do, God does; what man cannot give, God gives; what man cannot redeem, God redeems. But we must note that in this self-giving action of God for men God himself is involved. He

does not send out a chosen servant, as a football manager might send out a 'substitute' ten minutes from the end of the match in order to snatch a winning goal, but God enters the action personally. Why? A drastic situation requires a drastic remedy. The disruption of God's world by sin, the helplessness of man to redeem man, the spoiling of human relations through man's greed and evil, the awful separation between God and man, the despair in the heart of man, all this and more drove the Son of God to his cross. To stay with the letter to the Hebrews for a little longer, the writer argues that it is because Jesus is God's Son that he can also be the high priest among men and offer a full sacrifice to meet the penalty of sin. In Hebrews, and for that matter, in many other parts of the New Testament, the image of blood is used to convey the message of salvation. Images like 'blood' and 'sacrifices' may not be very appealing to modern people and not too readily recognizable as meaningful symbols of deliverance, but there is no mistaking the message. Blood symbolizes Christ's death. 'He entered once for all into the Holy Place, taking not the blood of goats and calves but his own blood, thus securing redemption . . . how much more shall the blood of Christ . . . purify your conscience from dead works' (Heb. 9:12–14). Here is the length to which God was prepared to go in sending his Son. Jesus was prepared to go to his cross as a 'blasphemer' against the law, as a 'rebel' against the status quo and as 'God-forsaken', to use Moltmann's description,[8] because there was no other way of demonstrating to the world that, in this rejection, the final showdown between God and man had begun.

Secondly, it bears witness to the love of God. In Hebrews the argument is that Old Testament ritual was ineffective because the high priest was a sinner also. He could represent sinners but he could not represent God. Furthermore, the ordained means of atonement, blood of bulls and goats, could not make moral atonement for the sins of men. The startling thing is that God even provides the victim needed to redeem mankind, 'his own Son'. St John Chrysostom rightly remarks, 'God showed what the human soul is worth when he did not spare his own Son'.[9] The Son of God is therefore both priest and victim, sharing the nature of both, and we can say truly that it is all of God. And it has to be if it must retain the character of an eternal sacrifice. It must have the validation of God's seal, and what greater seal can there be than that it is God's Son who died for men?

Jesus, Son of God, Saviour

'The mystery of the Incarnation', wrote Karl Barth, 'unfolds into the mystery of Good Friday and Easter'.[10] Here at this point of salvation not only is the purpose of Christ's ministry revealed but his real nature as well. What gives significance to the humiliation of the cross is not the fact that a man dies, but that this man is God's Son who bears the insults and rejection of men. In the following triumph of Easter Day the mystery is not so much that God is triumphant but that man is raised up too in Christ to take his place with God. Held together in tension these two elements tell the amazing story that an exchange has taken place. God becomes man and dies for humanity so that man in repentance is raised with Christ to the heavenly places!

A mystery; and so it is. In Dillistone's beautiful book *Jesus Christ and His Cross* he mentions that someone once asked the incomparable dancer Pavlova what she meant by a certain dance which she had performed. The great dancer replied, 'Do you think I would have *danced* it if I could have *said* it?'[11] There is a sense in which the cross defies all human explanation and searching. I don't mean to suggest that it is meaningless; far from it. Mystery is not the same as meaninglessness. The cross at many different levels makes sense in terms of justice, mercy, love and forgiveness. But if it is not meaningless, it is certainly mysterious. Why God chose *this* way no one can tell; but that it was his way we do not doubt. Perhaps the greater mystery is that God becomes incarnate to save men from their sins. And yet, no other explanation will do. If we approach Jesus as man we shall have great difficulty in explaining *why* his death should have more efficacy than that of any other great figure of the past. But if we approach him as the Scriptures do, and as the early church did, as Son of God and Lord, then his work of salvation becomes coherent to us and coherent *within* theology as a whole.

In this chapter we have concentrated upon the relationship between Jesus' work and his person. We have argued that unless we hold together the unity between *who* he is and *what* he did we seriously distort the gosepl of Christ. In a way we have to risk speaking of an incarnate-atonement because it is one movement, one action, of God who redeems.

6
Jesus, the Unique and Final Revelation of God?

It is easy to assert the uniqueness of Christianity when there are no other rivals around. Up to recent times the existence of other religions has been a fact all western Christians have recognized but few have experienced personally. We sent missionaries overseas and we sang hymns such as:

'Let the song go round the earth,
Lands where Islam's sway
Darkly broods o'er home and hearth,
Cast their bonds away . . .'

The position, however, has changed quite remarkably. The ease of modern travel has led a growing number of people from the East to trade with, and to study in, the West, and they have brought with them the flavour and the distinctiveness of their religion and culture. And to our surprise they do not seem all that 'dark' or depraved! Perhaps of even greater significance over the last couple of decades has been the resurgence of eastern religions leading to widespread missionary renewal, with the result that rivals to Christ have been established not just in Benares and Baghdad but also in Birmingham and Regent's Park. For nearly 1500 years since Constantine made Christianity the official religion of the Roman Empire it has had no serious rival; now it is in the market-place of faiths; one on offer among many. The question whether it is fundamentally different from other great world religions is increasingly being raised by theologians.

According to Professor John Hick it is not fundamentally different. In his book, *God and the Universe of Faiths* he challenges the uniqueness of Christ and calls for a 'Copernican Revolution' in theology to abandon the notion that outside Christianity there is no salvation. The doctrine that Christianity is at the centre of faith must go, so as to put 'God at the centre,' . . . 'all the religions of mankind, including our own, serve and revolve around him'.[1] What then of the conflicting claims made by the religions; can we assess their respective merits and truths? Hick replies that God transcends the human mind and that the different understandings of him represent genuine encounters with the divine reality from different historical and cultural standpoints.[2] Christianity, like other religions, is a 'human creation' whose history is part of the wider history of human culture.[3] In chapter 2, Professor Hick explores what this means for the doctrine of the incarnation. The traditional idea of *'homoousios'* (Christ's shared nature with the Father) should be understood not in terms of substance but of activity, in particular, the activity of love. God was incarnate in the sense that in Jesus the love of God was fully expressed. If we say more than that then we move into the realm of myth. All the doctrines associated with the doctrine of the incarnation have the function of expressing the believer's conviction that it is through this man Jesus and no other that he has experienced God. In just the same way, and just as appropriately, the Muslim will say the same of the Qur'an. Hick argues that had Christianity spread eastwards instead of westwards its intellectual formulation would have been different; Jesus would not have been regarded as the unique incarnation of God but rather as one among many 'Bodhisattvas', having attained to oneness with Ultimate Reality. In his most recent publication, *The*

Myth of God Incarnate, he repudiates the incarnation even more strongly, as excessively 'parochial' and as a barrier to dialogue and growth with other faiths. Other religions must be seen as legitimate avenues of salvation and we cannot say that 'all who are saved are saved by Jesus of Nazareth'.[4] He appeals for a global religious vision which makes sense of the diversity of God's ways with men. Incarnation, as traditionally understood, is an obstacle to this ideal.

We must observe carefully that Professor Hick's 'reconstructed theology' springs from the conviction that there is little distinctive about Christianity. All the great world religions are valid cultural expressions which arise from different social contexts. The radical re-interpretation of Jesus and all that flows from him is secondary to the desire for a global religious vision. Christ comes second to World Religions.

It is of course true that Christianity must come to terms with the existence of other religions, not merely because they now present missionary challenge to the mission of the church but also because there is much we can learn from them. Frank recognition of the wealth of other faiths should be given as well as appreciation of their contribution towards humanity as a whole. Christians have not always embodied the loving example of their Lord in his relationships with others; sometimes Christians in non-Christian contexts have been too quick to dismiss or reject anything that belongs to an alien faith. There is, indeed, much we can learn from other faiths, and Hick is surely right in suggesting that we too can be spiritually enriched by God's gifts mediated through them.

But it is unfair to other religions, as it is to Christianity itself, to ignore the distinctiveness of the Christian faith. Hick's analysis of Christianity is a serious travesty of the Christian message in the way he ignores, almost entirely, the way Jesus has shaped it. The church does not, and must not, apologize for the fact that it regards Jesus Christ as wholly unique and that it wants all men to know him and to follow him.

The scandal of particularity

It must be said clearly, yet with charity, that the Christian faith cannot surrender the claim that God in Christ has disclosed himself in a particular way at a particular moment in time. Christianity stands or falls with the belief that it was God himself in the form of a man who trod this earth, suffered with and for men, and who died for them on the cross. We should not minimize, or blur, the stark difference between Christianity and other faiths on this point of God becoming man.

First, the scandal is that of speaking, as Christians must, in terms of the incarnation as a unique historical event in which God intervened decisively in the world he had created. The Muslim parts company with us at this point, because although he has a high regard for Jesus as a prophet and as a man of God, the notion that God was localized in Jesus, or any person for that matter, is a blasphemous and idolatrous idea. Incarnation finds no place within the structures of such a rigid monotheism. Neither is it acceptable to the Hindu, although in the Avatar faith of Hinduism we have the closest approximation to the Christian doctrine of incarnation. The avatar is the appearance of a divine being on earth, but even here we find grave differences. H. D. Lewis points out, 'An avatar may enter human life but he does not share it, he is over it'.[5] Not only are some of the avatars sub-human, but even those in human form are only wearing a disguise and not a full human nature like that of Jesus. Now it is certainly true that Jesus' incarnation would be acceptable to the Hindu but not the argument that it is unique or final.[6] It is quite easy for a Hindu to accept Christ as yet another incarnation of the deity, but to give him a supreme throne would be anathema. Hick argues that there are remarkable similarities between Buddhology and Christology[7] and there certainly are, but as Parrinder points out the similarities are more apparent than real. In Buddhism the emphasis falls upon Buddha's reincarnation for more than five hundred lives. Even if one granted the use of the term incarnation to the last reincarnation of Buddha, it is never believed that this was God manifested in the flesh. 'If Nirvana is the divine substitute, he is hardly Nirvana-become-flesh.'[8] There is a world of difference between the passive and serene figure of Buddha and the active, suffering figure of Christ.

This indeed takes us into the second area, that of suffering and death. From a non-Christian perspective Christianity makes an outrageous claim when it asserts that in this man Jesus God himself went to a lonely cross. The Muslim finds this totally unacceptable. In the Qur'an Jesus the prophet does not die on the cross but he is taken by God. For the Buddhist or Hindu the crucified Jesus is a meaningless and sometimes gruesome symbol of suffering. Parrinder speaks of a Buddhist who gives voice to the revulsion he felt on entering a Christian church and seeing the image of a naked man bleeding and dying on a cross. 'I cannot help thinking of the gap that lies deep between christianity and buddhism. The crucified Christ is a terrible sight and I cannot help associating it with the sadistic impulse of a psychically affected brain'.[9] For the Buddhist there can be no detached calm nor spiritual elevation in contemplating such a disturbing image.

But the incarnation is not something that the Christian should be ashamed of, or want to apologize for; it should be, on the contrary, his great joy that God has revealed himself so completely in his Son and it is he that the church desires to share with the rest of the world.

The scandal of salvation through Jesus only

As we noted earlier, Hick views traditional statements about Jesus as forming barriers to the creation of a pan-religious movement, and he appeals for a rejection of exclusive claims made on Jesus' behalf. But the Jesus of the

New Testament cannot be bound in this way. If he is not a universal saviour he is not a saviour at all. It will not do for Christian proclamation to be restricted to the Christian world. His ministry is as wide as creation and he comes to claim all men as his own and he demands universal acknowledgment as 'Lord'. There can be no rivals to his Lordship. Such is the clear testimony of the New Testament and this was the reason why so many Christians died for their faith. Compromise and tolerance of other systems of belief would have made Christianity perfectly acceptable in the early period of the church. But Christians went about their business believing that, although there may be so-called gods . . . yet for us there is one God, the Father . . . and one Lord, Jesus Christ' (1 Cor. 8:5,6).

In claiming the world for Jesus Christ and allowing no diminution of his significance we must emphasize that this is not a cry for a crude programme of evangelism which plants the same formula regardless of country and culture. If he is proclaimed as saviour and Lord it must be done within the culture and in accord with the religious ideas and thought-forms of that society. God does work through and in other faiths and we should expect him to be preparing the way for Christ in those societies where Christ is being proclaimed.

But when Jesus Christ is accepted as Lord a certain displacing of ideas must take place which, from the outsider's viewpoint, seems to be a rejection of all that has gone before. First, Christ takes the place of eminence in a person's life over everything else. Symbolized in baptism, it declares a break with the past and the commencement of a new life. But it is not necessarily a complete rejection of the past. Many new Christians from other faiths have viewed their new faith not as being discontinuous from their original beliefs but as a natural completion of them. Secondly, the Christian faith introduces new understandings of God to deepen those already understood within his own inherited faith. One of the most important is that of God as 'Father'.

No longer conceived of as 'out there', far removed from the trials of life, God is now understood and experienced as 'Abba'. Indeed, this teaching of God as Father in a personal sense is one of the most distinctive features over against other religions. The struggle for possession by the 'divine' or 'illumination' finds its fulfilment in a personal relationship with a heavenly Father. We are not meant to be God or to become in any way divine, but we are expected to have an abiding destiny in an abiding relation with him.

But it is most probably in Jesus Christ's universal ministry of meeting people's needs as saviour from sin which outlines the difference between Christianity and non-Christian faiths. Hick is surely right when he says that 'the Christian gift to the world is Jesus'.[10] But he is a gift only in so far as he confronts men as the Way, Truth and Life. Herein lies the difference for example between Buddha and Christ. Apparently Buddha, when he was dying, was asked by his disciples how they should remember him. He replied that his followers should not trouble themselves about such a question. It did not matter whether he was remembered or not. What mattered was the teaching which, if lived fully, would lead them to illumination and release. The 'way' was almost like a scientific teaching. It did not matter who propounded it as long as it was used. But this is not the Christian perspective. Jesus is not merely a teacher but a redeemer. He draws people to him, and his community is a community of people who have met him as redeemer. As we have more than once mentioned, Christ cannot be understood apart from his work as saviour. As mediator, he stands between God and man, the expression of the inexhaustible love of God, and as the fulfilment of mankind's eternal destiny when they respond to him. As saviour, he stands between God and man not as one saviour among many but as the *only* way of salvation. So John's Gospel declares: 'God so loved the world that he gave his only Son that whoever believes in him should not perish but have eternal life' (Jn. 3:16). Of course, it is not for us to set limits to God's love. The loving God of the New Testament 'desires all men to be saved' (1 Tim. 2:4). We must allow that the God of all grace may work in his own way among those who have never heard the matchless name of Jesus. But we must add, whoever is saved, whether he is within the church or outside it, is not saved because of his religion or because of his goodness but is saved only through Jesus Christ, the only saviour and mediator. This doctrine attacks all systems of self-salvation, all systems of merit, and all systems of 'illumination' which depend on the holiness and goodness of their adherents. Although the sense of sin is not as strong in eastern religion as it is in Christianity, its power is still felt and people are still in its bondage. Winslow quotes a common Indian saying, 'I came to Allahabad; I washed, but my sins came away with me'.[11] The sovereign remedy resides in Christ. It consists of the coming of God to the very heart of the human situation, to endure the suffering of humanity in a fully human life, and to die for all men on a 'God-forsaken' cross. For that reason we can say boldly with Stephen Neill about the cross: 'For the human sickness there is one specific remedy and this is it. There is no other'.[12]

The finality of Jesus

Hick is quite correct, however, to see the incarnation of Jesus as a stumbling-block to the formation of a global fellowship of religions bound together in a federation of good-will. It is not that the idea of incarnation is offensive; the offence lies in its tacit declaration that in Christ God's revelation is found finally and completely. Sir Norman Anderson points out that 'If God could have *adequately* revealed himself in any other way, how can one possibly believe he would have gone to the almost unbelievable lengths of the incarnation?'[13] In becoming man God embodies the finality of the revelation in Christ. So the letter to the Hebrews begins, 'In many and various ways God spoke of old to our fathers by the prophets; but in these last days he has spoken to us by a Son'. This forms the basis for the writer's appeal to his readers not to go back to their former faith which foreshadowed the coming of Christ. In other passages of Scripture the finality of Christ is worked out more closely. In the letter to the Ephesians for example the idea of the divine plan culminating in the appearance of Jesus expresses the Pauline idea most clearly. Before the foundation of the world, God elected Christians to receive sonship through Jesus Christ (Eph. 1:13,14). His eternal plan was to unite all things in him, things in heaven and things on earth (v.10). Here the universal significance of Jesus is that everything with which God's plan has to do will find him as its centre and goal.

With the finality of Christ there goes, of course, the finality of his message. A hint of this is given by Christ himself when he declares that 'no one knows the Father except the Son and any one to whom the Son chooses to reveal him' (Mt. 11:27). The same uncompromising idea is taken up in John 14:6 where Christ states that 'I am the way, and the truth, and the life; no one comes to the Father but by me'. As the only way to the Father he becomes the subject of the apostolic preaching and Peter declares that 'there is salvation in no one else, for there is no other name under heaven given among men by which we must be saved' (Acts 4:12). What is more, Christ's salvation is seen as the final offer to men. So the letter to the Hebrews states that 'he has appeared once for all at the end of the age to put away sin by sacrifice of himself, (9:26). It is evident that here, as in many other passages in the New Testament, the writers assumed that with Christ the end of the world was near. But however long the end-times, their confident belief was that in Christ's death on the cross God had spoken decisively and finally. These are some of the explicit testimonies to Christ as the fulfilment of men, but the implicit testimony of the New Testament is no less clear with its firm teaching of Christ as the 'end' of the law, and the fulfilment of the prophets and the conviction that the last judgment would revolve around whether or not Jesus Christ was their saviour. But some would retort, 'Must we be bound by documents nearly two thousand years old? Shouldn't the spirit of Christ govern our attitudes to other faiths, the spirit of love and tolerance?' The spirit of Christ must govern our thinking and our faith at all times, but unless we have very good reason to believe that the testimony of the New Testament is not reflecting his will, we are committed for better or worse to its testimony, and thus committed to proclaim it just as firmly and confidently as the first disciples did.

We are still left with the scandal of the message we proclaim. For this we must make no apology. If we believe that Jesus Christ is God's own Son then we must go on to proclaim that in him we and all mankind find our true being and salvation. In this, compromise is not possible, even to please those of other faiths, or to suit the relativism of scholars such as Hick and others. This must not be taken as narrow-minded exclusivism, because we do not want to exclude but to invite all to share the riches of Christ which we enjoy; but it is a frank recognition of his unique claims upon all. The supreme gift we bring to others, not arrogantly nor with pride, is that in Jesus our Lord we find the final and complete answer to man's needs. We say indeed with H. D. Lewis that 'He came in complete human form to meet a universal need in a way that is adequate for all times and places and is without parallel or substitute'.[14]

7

A Gospel to Preach?

Throughout this booklet we have kept before us two positions. On the one hand there is a radical view which treats Jesus as a man and not a divine being and the incarnation as a false interpretation of New Testament teaching. On the other side there is the classical view which sees Jesus as a divine person who assumes human nature, and the incarnation as a truth which must be adhered to at all costs because it is the central tenet of Christianity.

But as is patently obvious this is not a theological game of Rads v. Trads! And it is certainly not a case of 'you pays your money and you takes your choice'. What is at stake is the relevance, and even the continuance, of the gospel in the modern world. One of the leading theologians on the radical side, Professor John Hick, sees this very clearly and this is at the heart of his theology, I believe. He wants the Christian faith to be meaningful to modern people, and his desire is that the central figure of Christianity, Jesus himself, should be there for all to see. One does not impugn the motives of scholars like him, neither does one doubt their sincerity. But sincerity is not enough. The question really is 'Is the message we believe, whatever it may be, preachable? Is it a basis for living? Is it true?'

The question does not merely ask, 'Is that what I believe today, as I sit in my study or armchair?' but 'Am I committed enough to it to live it, preach it and die for it?' If we push the implications a little further we could go on to ask 'Do we believe that others would be convinced by it too?' 'Is it preachable?' is the acid test which must be applied to any reformulated faith. Has it enough content to warrant whole-hearted confidence?

The radical position calls us to accept a reductionist gospel which is pruned of difficulties for modern man and counter-faiths. Possibly it has just enough content to be called Christian, although if it were accepted and believed the creeds and liturgies of the Churches would have to be changed. Take the creed said in Anglican Churches every Sunday: 'The only begotten Son of God, begotten of his Father before all worlds, God of God, light of light, very God of very God . . . who for us men and for our salvation came down from heaven . . . incarnate by the Holy Ghost of the Virgin Mary; and was made man'. That would certainly have to go! And when we come to the Prayer of Thanksgiving, the section about 'through him you created all things from the beginning' would have to be changed, as indeed, most of the prayer, because its triumphant assertions are only made and only ring true with the assumption that his death, resurrection, ascension and second coming are unique events with eternal significance.

The question 'Is it preachable?' is, however, more important than the effects of a radical view of Christ upon the worshipping life of the church, because the future of Christianity is at stake with the answer given. Now when we focus the question upon Jesus stripped of divinity, who differed from us only by degree, who may, or may not, have been the most wonderful human being of all time, we begin to doubt whether we know that much about him or his teaching to get very excited. If I doubt the New Testament's testimony about him, what sound reasons have I to believe that this wonderful being is of relevance to us today? I also happen to believe that Marcus Aurelius was a wonderful man who wrote some inspiring things, who lived a good life, some would say an exemplary life, who epitomized in his personal tragedy the suffering of the world in which he lived. But Marcus Aurelius is dead. His teaching is interesting, but of only marginal help to us today because it is shaped by the age in which he lived. It belongs back there with him.

Furthermore, we could ask, can the radical gospel be preached with enthusiasm and conviction by men and women gripped by the love of Christ and convinced that he is of inestimable importance to people today? There is no evidence, as far as I can see, that this is happening. A reduced doctrine of Christ is very difficult to preach because uncertainty is the basis from which it works.

The New Testament gospel cannot really be reduced. Its message is that, in Jesus of Nazareth, God has come to meet every man in every generation to face them with his unconditional claims and his unreserved love. He came once for all, long ago, as a man and he lived and died for the salvation of all. His triumphant resurrection from the tomb signals his victory over death and the forces of evil which hold men in bondage. His church is built on this rock and his promise is that nothing can prevail against it. His incarnation is not a luxury with which we can dispense because it is uncomfortable to us, or because it is offensive to others. It is essential to all that we do today as Christians.

Take our personal discipleship. The incarnation speaks of God's involvement in human nature, tempted yet victorious over sin; his involvement with people who loved him yet turned against him; his concern for lost people in a lost world. If he were just a man, separated from us by the splendour of a matchless life, this would not make it any easier for us in our daily pilgrimage. If he is matchless, or wonderful, a great gulf separates the ordinary and failing person from such a one. Despair must set in because, however inspiring or noble the example, unless that person knows how I feel and knows me intimately, his splendid example is as far removed as Michelangelo's paintings are from my small daughter's blobs. The incarnation, however, does not speak of separation but of God's identity with us and for us. Jesus remains God but enters into the indignity of human existence. That's love for you.

Take our salvation. The incarnation testifies to God's total commitment to his world. He is not involved from the outside in the life of a man from Galilee; he does not watch the proceedings with detached interest as you and I might watch the International Horse Show, but he comes among us to save. The incarnation stands as a symbol that, in Jesus, God has dealt with sin and guilt and has taken mankind's burdens completely upon his shoulders. That's good news for anyone!

Take the world religions. The incarnation speaks of God's great love for all men, a love which drove Jesus to the lonely frontier of separation from his Father and his friends and to a death which no one else could share. That incarnation drives his people to go themselves to the world's end, and to other frontiers of need and despair, for the love of him who did not count his life dear to himself. As Christ says himself in John's Gospel, 'As the Father has sent me, even so I send you' (Jn. 20:21). There is an essential identity between the incarnation and the proclamation of Christ in the world. The one who sent becomes the one who sends, and he can send his people to suffering and death only because he also, having left all, has walked the pathway of obedience.

We do not mean to suggest that the Christian has a neat and tidy gospel which is problem-free. The gospel is lived in the world and it has to be related to the needs of our time. We do not know all the answers or, for that matter, all the questions! It is right that we should study carefully radical approaches to the Christian faith as well as listen to the questions and doubts of the secular world in which we are set and which we are committed to serve. But we would say that the gospel must not be merely talked about but lived out. A theological system has little right to be called by that noble name if it has not been tested in the world. Words and ideas cost nothing; and they mean nothing unless we can prove that they work.

Our responsibility to our generation is to proclaim the living Christ in intelligent ways based upon the unchanging nature of our gospel. Our understanding of Christ must be adequate for a continuing and living world-wide church. Only an understanding grounded firmly in the bed-rock of incarnation, that God became flesh and dwelt among us, has sufficient strength as well as support from the Scriptures to stand the test of time.

Notes

Chapter 1
[1] J. Hick, ed., *The Myth of God Incarnate* (SCM, 1977).

Chapter 2
[1] J. Hick, *Christianity at the Centre* (SCM Centre book, 1968), p. 19.
[2] C. E. B. Cranfield, *The Gospel According to St. Mark* (Cambridge University Press), p. 157.
[3] Hick, *Myth*, p. 52.
[4] Ibid., p. 172.
[5] J. Hick, *Daily Mail*, 29 June 1977.
[6] Hick, *Myth*, p. 132.
[7] Ibid., p. 52.
[8] Hick, *Christianity*, p. 18.
[9] A. M. Hunter, *Bible and Gospel* (SCM, 1969), p. 59.
[10] Hick, *Myth*, p. 56.
[11] Hunter, *Bible*, p. 133.
[12] Hick, *Myth*, p. 8.
[13] Ibid., p. 54.
[14] Ibid., p. 57.
[15] Ibid., p. 60.

Chapter 3
[1] J. Jeremias, *Theology of the New Testament I* (SCM), p. 54.
[2] I. Howard Marshall, *The Origins of New Testament Christology* (IVP, 1977), p. 116.
[3] H. Küng, *On Being a Christian* (Collins, 1977), p. 344.
[4] G. Ladd, *I Believe in the resurrection of Jesus Christ* (Hodder, 1975).
[5] E. M. B. Green, *Man Alive!* (IVP, 1967).
[6] Hick, *Myth*, p. 171.

Chapter 4
[1] C. F. D. Moule, *Commentary on*

Colossians (Cambridge University Press), p. 59.
[2]F. Young in *The Myth of God Incarnate,* ed. J. Hick.
[3]For examples see C. H. Dodd, *The Historical Tradition in the Fourth Gospel* (1963).
C. L. Mitton, *Jesus: The facts behind the Faith* (Eerdmans, 1973).
R. Brown, *The Gospel According to St. John* (Anchor Bible), I.
L. Morris, *Studies in the Fourth Gospel* (Paternoster Press, 1969).
[4]Hick, *Myth,* p. 81.

Chapter 5

[1]In *The Crucified God* by J. Moltmann (SCM, 1975), p. 85.
[2]*Origen Against Celsus,* Bk. VI, Ch. XLVII.
[3]J. A. Robinson, *The Human Face of God* (SCM, 1973), p. 179.
[4]Ibid., p. 194.
[5]Hick, *Myth,* p. 59.
[6]H. E. W. Turner, *Jesus the Christ* (Mowbrays, 1976), p. 95.
[7]P. T. Forsyth, *The Person and Place of Jesus Christ* (London, 1909), p. 76.
[8]J. Moltmann, *The Crucified God,* p. 130ff.

[9]St. John Crysostom, *Commentary on Matthew 18.*
[10]K. Barth, *Dogmatics in Outline* (SCM, 1949), p. 114.
[11]F. W. Dillistone, *Jesus and His Cross* (Lutterworth, 1952), p. 139.

Chapter 6

[1]*God and the Universe of Faiths* (Macmillan, 1973), p. 131.
[2]Ibid., p. 143.
[3]Ibid., p. 101.
[4]Hick, *Myth,* p. 181.
[5]H. D. Lewis and R. L. Slater, *World Religions* (C. A. Watts & Co., 1966), p. 186.
[6]G. Parrinder, *Avatar and Incarnation* (Faber, 1970), p. 231.
[7]Hick, *Myth,* p. 169.
[8]Parrinder, *Avatar,* p. 247.
[9]Ibid., p. 214.
[10]Hick, *Myth,* p. 182.
[11]J. Winslow, *The Christian Approach to the Hindu.*
[12]S. Neill, *Christian Faith and Other Faiths* (OUP, 1961), p. 16.
[13]Sir Norman Anderson, *Christianity and Comparative Religion* (IVP, 1970).
[14]Lewis and Slater, *World Religions,* p. 193.

Crossroads College
G.H. Cachiaras Memorial Library
920 Mayowood Road SW, Rochester MN 55902
507-535-3331

For Further Reading

*Berkouwer, G. C. *The Person of Christ.* England: Inter-Varsity Press, 1974.

Denney, J. *The Death of Christ.* InterVarsity Press, 1951.

Forsyth, P. T. *The Person and Place of Jesus Christ.* London, 1909.

France, R. T. *I Came to Set the Earth on Fire: A Portrait of Jesus.* Inter-Varsity Press, 1975.

Green, E. M. B., ed. *The Truth of God Incarnate.* Eerdmans, 1977.

Hunter, A. M. *Bible and Gospel.* SCM, 1969.

Jeremias, J. *The Central Message of the New Testament.* SCM, 1965.

Ladd, G. E. *Jesus and the Kingdom.* SPCK, 1964.

Marshall, I. Howard. *The Origins of New Testament Christology.* InterVarsity Press, 1977.

McDonald, H. D. *Jesus: Human and Divine.* Pickering and Inglis, 1968.

Morris, L. *The Lord from Heaven.* InterVarsity Press, 1958.

*Moule, C. F. D. *The origins of Christology.* Cambridge University Press, 1977.

Muggeridge, M. *Another King.* St. Andrew Press, 1968.

*Pannenberg, W. *Jesus, God and Man.* SCM, 1968.

Ramsey, A. M. *The Glory of God and the Transfiguration of Christ.* London, 1949.

Turner, H. E. W. *Jesus, Master and Lord.* Mowbrays, 1953.

Zahrnt, H. *The historical Jesus.* Collins, 1963.

*For more advanced study.